IS, IS NOT

Also by Tess Gallagher

POETRY

Boogie-Woogie Crisscross (with Lawrence Matsuda)
Midnight Lantern: New and Selected Poems
Dear Ghosts,
My Black Horse: New and Selected Poems
Portable Kisses
Moon Crossing Bridge
Amplitude: New and Selected Poems
Willingly
Under Stars
Instructions to the Double

FICTION

The Man from Kinvara: Selected Stories
Barnacle Soup: Stories from the West of Ireland (with Josie Gray)
At the Owl Woman Saloon
The Lover of Horses and Other Stories

ESSAYS

Beyond Forgetting: Poetry and Prose about Alzheimer's Disease
     (edited by Holly J. Hughes, introduction by Tess Gallagher)
Soul Barnacles: Ten More Years with Ray (edited by Greg Simon)
A Concert of Tenses: Essays on Poetry
Carver Country (photographs by Bob Adelman, introduction
     by Tess Gallagher)
A New Path to the Waterfall (Raymond Carver, introduction
     by Tess Gallagher)
Alfredo Arreguin's World of Wonders: Critical Perspectives
     ("Viva La Vida" by Tess Gallagher)
All of Us (Raymond Carver, introduction by Tess Gallagher)

TRANSLATION

A Path to the Sea: Poems by Liliana Ursu (with Adam J. Sorkin and
     the poet, translator's note by Tess Gallagher)
Marina Tsvetaeva: The Essential Poetry (introduction by
     Tess Gallagher)
The Sky behind the Forest: Selected Poems by Liliana Ursu (with
     Adam J. Sorkin and the poet)

Tess Gallagher

IS, IS NOT

BLOODAXE BOOKS

ISBN: 978 1 78037 461 1

First published 2019
in the UK by
Bloodaxe Books Ltd,
Eastburn,
South Park,
Hexham,
Northumberland NE46 1BS,
and in North America
by Graywolf Press.

www.bloodaxebooks.com
For further information about Bloodaxe titles
please visit our website and join our mailing list
or write to the above address for a catalogue.

Supported using public funding by
**ARTS COUNCIL
ENGLAND**

Book design: Rachel Holscher.
Cover painting: Josie Gray, *Blue Eyelid Lifting*
Cover design: Neil Astley & Pamela Robertson-Pearce.
Composition: Bookmobile Design and Digital Publisher Services, Minneapolis.

Printed in Great Britain by Bell & Bain Limited, Glasgow, Scotland, on
acid-free paper sourced from mills with FSC chain of custody certification.

for Josie Gray and for Raymond Carver

CONTENTS

RECOGNITION

Staring down from the bridge
at the moon
broken up
in the river, who
could know, without looking
up, it stands whole above
                    its shattered self.

i

Am I real? Do I exist?
And will I really die?

OSIP MANDELSTAM

In the Company of Flowers

all day, coming away
like an ordinary person who
might have been at a till. Thinking
as I dug into earth of my mother
who, when my youngest brother
died, was taken in
by beauty, not as consolation
but because she found him
there as she made the garden.

Each day she tended it
he kept a little more
of her. If ever I doubt
the power of the dead, I walk
her garden in May, rhododendrons
so red, so white their clustered goblets
spill translucent tongues of light at the rim
of the sea. And it is ordinary

to be so accompanied,
so fused to the silence of all that,
as it eludes me, as I am taken in.

Surely my reappearance must wear
the borrowed abundance she
gave me that morning
I was born.

Almost Lost Moment

coming back in an incidental way,
claiming to be *the most beautiful*
moment of my life: braiding
her waist-length white hair by the Pacific
at La Push. Hand over
hand, the three-way crossings
of apportioned strands, and quiet,
her head braced against my gentle pull
as she gazes out. Both in our sea-minds.
And quiet.
Quiet.

for Georgia Morris Bond,
my mother

AMBITION

We had our heads down
baiting hooks—three wild salmon
already turned back that morning
for the in-season hatchery silvers
now out there somewhere
counting their luck—when
under our small boat the sea
gave a roll like a giant turning over

in sleep, lifting us high so I thought
an ocean liner or freighter had
slipped up on us, the sudden heft
of its bow-wave, our matchstick toss
to depth we'd taken
for granted in order to venture there
at all. But when I looked up expecting
collision, the quash of water from their

blowholes pushed to air in unison,
a pair of gray whales not two hundred
yards away: "Look up!" I shouted so you
didn't miss the fear-banishing
of their passage that made
nothing of us. Not even death could touch
any mind of us. It was all beauty and
mystery, the kind that picks you up

effortlessly and darts through you
for just those moments
you aren't even there. Held that way
and their tons-weight bodies plunged

silently under again, I turned for proof
to you, but the clarity was passing through
as a swell under us again and the sky of the sea
set us down like a toy.

And that's the way it was, and it wasn't
any other way—just looking at each other,
helpless one thought and huge with power
the next. We baited up,
dropped our herring into slack water—
two ghosts fishing for anything but whales.

for my brother Tom

YOUR DOG PLAYING WITH A COYOTE

—a notion not out of place
where bears hunch under apple
trees at night like rocking chairs
with volition. She's lonely, your dog,
and the young coyote waits for her at the edge
of the forest. Not sinister that tongue

laughing wildness when she
dashes forward to feign attack, then glances
away. If your dog chases too far,
what then? Joining wilder kin to rove
at borders suddenly treacherous? What does
dusk have to do with their marauding?

Some ancient tincture of permission
allows the edge of night
to blend where wild and tame
exchange fur in one naked, human
mind—my thinking toward them
to grant wilderness its emissary.
Coyote, whose very appearance takes

whisper to its highest pitch—then breaks
the play-form of invitation to withdraw,
shedding with a guiltless, backward
look, this unbidden fringe-work—to rejoin
her serial moons, her black on black
of night, our freshened
immensity.

Ability to Hold Territory

The chilla is the fox Charles Darwin
killed by walking up and hitting it
on the head with a hammer
while it was "intently watching
the activity" of the *Beagle*'s crew.

Notoriously unwary of humans, "It
doesn't know to hide from hunters."
In effect, it steps off the ladder
of evolution where "ability to hold territory
supersedes ability to adapt
to environmental changes."

~

The women huddle in the Men's
in the Turkish airport. Gun shots
ring out, then massive explosions. Escaping
down a stairwell, the talisman
of a woman's scarf, then a smeared
footprint where blood outleaped
its borders.

~

It wasn't the first time a wrongheaded
freedom had taken the floor
of our assembly. The surprise was
that the head actually rolled down the aisle
toward my bench where my foot
took hold of me and kicked it
mercilessly out the door.

~

Now we are all tossed out
into straw, or worse,
a ditch. I study my watch as if
a mistake in time would
repeal what was inconceivable
only days before. Hammer

of the mind, come down
on the glass of this hour, and
spread alarm! Each choice
does small or large harm, but
to do nothing is to cease
to exist and banish worlds.

BLIND DOG/SEEING GIRL

She travels by guess and by
mistakes she corrects
by going back the wrong
way, bumping sometimes
painfully into things with her
whole face like houses and
tree trunks and door
jambs. She can't get there

except by correction, extending
her chin against the stairs as if
they were the stars, to caress
each oncoming cement
ledge. If she didn't venture
and get it wrong and eventually
right, she'd be at a standstill, marooned
out there under the apple trees or
hemlock. Don't

carry her, says the girl to
herself, you'll mix her up
in there in her dark-finding
where she's collecting
mistakes and self-forgiveness,
making good on excited passages
where it seems each turnabout
yields a fresh chance at getting back
to the girl. And what is the girl

for? To clap her hands helplessly over
and over and chant "This way! This

way!" And because the dog is also deaf,
the girl is there to follow her
to her neighbor's porch where
the dog scratches to be let
in. The girl is there to explain, to
apologize: "She's blind, she's deaf,"
and in quiet defeat to snap the lead

on the dog's collar and guide her home
where in relative safety she releases her
again into her lostness from which
the dog must design
a freedom-map among the galaxies
of blind orbits, brailled
edges, and comets of the moment.

Even the girl knows in her sighted
witnessing: we are each
lost, and beholden until,
with deer-like tentative stepping,
each invisible threshold yields, and
still calling in her useless voice,
the girl forfeits all notion of possessing
the zigzagged way her exactly *there* dog
at last hazards herself into

her waiting arms. And isn't it joy
the dog expresses as the world
dissolves into just that moment
she has magically united with
her very own missing girl.

Doe Browsing Salal Berries

My restraint in pruning allows
another harvest. Blue-black pearls
cling to flexible combs, bounty
her tongue searches out from
rhododendron leaves, all but
subsumed by salal. We exchange

a long *you-there* stare
before she edges her muzzle in again,
then lifts the right hoof,
flicking her ears to engage some
possibly threatening unseen.
The day will turn, night will come

over her. The way it knows
to leave everything where it was
as she moves like a shadow
with its own volition
back into her forest.

ii

Give my dream back,
raven! The moon you woke me to
is misted over.

UEJIMA ONITSURA

Little Inside Out Dream,

how real you are, bringing me
the morning glories of my
two old friends as young
on a full-moon night. How
sad-happy it was to embrace
them, for he was also my old
love, and she—his eventual
bride; but forget that since time

had slipped its knot—his
mother was dying; we were
thumping the dark of that
when moonlight ignited
our corner of fortunate
intersection, brailling the moment
with the memory-chill
of lilies, and my alive-again mother

braiding my hair the night before
to take the hurry out of a school
morning. How tightly she pulled
to the back of my head, as if
she were climbing a moon-ladder
into this faraway moment. Then
I handed her the silk ribbons, one
by one, to secure the ends

and to hide the rubber bands
doing the real job of holding. How
I loved those mother-hands!
And silk. And that you brought

your sorrow to me, even though
all we were to each other across time
was young and
abandoned by mothers.

DREAM CANCEL

There is no *in* to the dream,
though closing the eyes to go there
would seem entrance, an interior
that closes one over, the Russian dolls'
papier-mâché replicas hooding serial
invitations you have to accept.
For in sleep we do submit, and the notion
long held of "waking up" does not free us
if the dream-mind does its
handstand in the corner.

Relieved of "waking" as permission to
dismiss the second-class life
of the dream with its colorful
cargo of talking bears and the ogre
wearing the ruby amulet—we live
unrepentantly on gingerbread doorknobs
and edible glass, our child fears hand-in-hand
with child delights, while the dreamer

gets more brazen in the witness-box of
daylight: *Not real! Only a dream!*
Yet, the hands are sticky,
the tongue coiled to the memory
of molasses. *Oh stick your finger out*
of the cage of sleep, little girl, so we can
rub your finger bone! But the mind
in the corner with its skirt fallen
over its daylight cries *No!* then substitutes

a chicken bone. And if your brother
is eaten in another room, you somehow meet
down a long cavernous hallway
where the melting polar ice has sluiced you
together again. Is there something *real*
on the other side of "real" when the dream
fails to exceed or cancel itself? His gingerbread
hand clings eternally to yours as you tilt
and slide away from heartbeats, from breath
on the window pane, from proof and cunning—yet

you manage somehow to stay alive
in the same way the mind
abandons its corner to stand its head up,
allowing its dream worlds to glisten as particulate
vanishings. Still, the *you* of "you"
puts nothing aside or behind as it
enters the red core of the amulet
whose protective attributes
sustain the no-such-thing-as-dream,
the no-such-thing-as-awake. The mind

lays its head down, puts its hands
in its sleep-pockets, turns the day over like
a fried egg, saunters off into the sunrise,
into the vast on and on, whistling
like a day laborer.

STOLEN DRESS

I was walking through a vast darkness
in a dress studded with diamonds, the cloth
under them like chainmail—metallic,
form fitting like the sea to its horizon. I could
hear waves breaking on the shore and far off
concertina music drifting over the dunes. What
was I doing in high heels in sand in a diamond-studded

dress that had to be stolen? Fear washed
through me, as if one of those waves had
risen up and, against all the rules of waves,
splashed me from the shoulders
down. I was wet with diamonds and fear.
A small boat held offshore with its cold
yellow light pointing a long watery finger at me

while the stolen feeling of the dress sparkled
my location out into the universe. *Thief! Thief!*
came an interplanetary cry, causing me to
gaze up into the star-brilliant firmament,
for it wasn't just a sky anymore. It had
taken on biblical stature. How had I
gotten into this dress, these unruly

waves, this queasy feeling I would be
found out? *Time to run!* my heart said,
pumping away under its brocade
of diamonds. Strange vacancies had
accumulated after all my sleep-plundered
nights. *Thief!* came the cry again, as if
I should recognize myself. And I did.

I flung those high heels into the depths,
took up my newfound identity, and without
the least remorse, began to run those diamonds
right out of this world.

GLASS IMPRESSES

most as it breaks. Look
how placidly it held our milk
in childhood as we sucked on the universe,
missing our first breasts. The wine glass
accidently dashed to
the floor is instantly replaced
with another—the party must go on!

Someone a little drunk
swept it up, but next morning
a shark's tooth glinted
its half-smile from under
the refrigerator skirting. Thank
goodness no one wanted
ice cream in the barefoot
night. Little glass of my dreams—half
full, half empty—dream-glass—
I'm filling you to the top

with Russian vodka drinkers.
Let's see how long you'll hold out
against their heedless elbows, their
desperate wounding of the inevitable. If
I break myself open to one more day,
am I not more glass to last night's sleep
for how my dreams shine through me,
sweeping me up, then dashing me
with impeccable impunity?

Broken? No, shattered! Loan me
a shard of tomorrow, or give

what is spilling me its freedom-tongue
so that in the Meadow of the Dead
there will be no blade of grass
that doesn't call to the passing lovers
to lie down and try out their broken songs
above the bones, below the shadows
of the clouds.

HUMMINGBIRD-MIND

Flit, a useful word,
allowing one in, yet escape
from presence. If mind is
at least hinge
to body, its jade lantern
gives dart and hover

their difference—an arm
that wishes it were
a wing, air displaced
by a finger-length
of wit. We do not so much as argue
with the never-was as slip

its noose. Suck down
two-thirds of your body
weight in nectar and by nightfall
you are no heavier than a star
to anyone's gaze. A lantern
communing with the dark

takes memory to another level
and even when lifted high
cannot bother to care
it does not illumine
an ocean with its
flotilla of shore-prone boats.

ONE DEER AT DUSK

The hummingbirds are still
fumbling the feeder with
occasional dive-bombing
to show each other how easy it is
to slip a tongue into sweetness
while others fight for
priorities—who sips first or
longest, or who can sit
pensive without sipping
at all. They know less

about deer, their
magnetic noses trained
to the young red tips of
roses. Yet tongue-sheath
beaks would challenge
fiercely if they caught deer
mawing the blossoms
of their honeysuckle.

The stealth-step of the deer
seems wishing not to tear
the fabric of this easing down
of night, shadow entering
shadow. And dusk, which allows
us to gaze across the boundary
of night's oncoming dream of
possessing us entirely, has enabled

the deer, in its shuttlecock moment,
to let us watch ourselves

as a soft muzzle
caress and take teeth
to what we've never tasted,
then be ourselves
consumed, as if night's unsheathed
all-over talisman of where we came from

had entered us while a deer
and hummingbirds occupied
what must have been
the night-nest of one mind
choosing not to close
until each step of the barely visible deer
has blended with the last whir
of hummingbird, vanished.

iii

I hate Batyushkov's arrogance:
"What's the time?" they asked him
once. He answered, "Eternity."

OSIP MANDELSTAM

CORRECTION

When he drank, he who was silent
talked into the night, and early on
you could get anything you
asked for. I can't remember
what I asked for, only that he
called me *Queenie*, a sweet-bitter
name, for try as he might, it was hard

by his day-to-day earnings to keep
a queen, even a child-queen. Anciently
he would tell my brothers and me the dark
of the coal mines, some proof of his
delivery from one hell-life to another.
How could a child lift that? So much

of being young just raw listening, waiting
for life to catch up and add
meaning. Time gentled us both
so at last he could break through
to plead his case, that time I'd
come home from studies. I was
grown, full of plans that didn't

include him. The Queen was waiting tables,
skivvying for a Russian who
owned a pizza joint on the Ave—

one of three jobs to keep her
in food and classes. "If
I'd of known," my father said,
"I'd of helped you more."

He'd taken me up wrong, he
said. "I thought you were just
off to find a man"—spoken with his
'50s mind of things. Then, like
some accident of truth, tears,

and, face to face in that sudden earthly
moment, we could take our bearings
and enter the stumbling of the heart
with its stored-up light.

                            for my father, Leslie Bond

SULLY

It hurts me to think of you
under the ground.

JAIME SABINES

My view of you is always aerial
like time to a child who surrounds
everything with promise. I'm above
you like a ceiling fan and you—laid out
as my father described you—on the only flat
surface in the house, the kitchen table—like
a banquet to which everyone is invited
but to which no one can sit
down. For the record, my father told us

your death as if it were the heaviest
grief of his young life. He'd been away working
in the Iowa coal mines, then come home on a whim
to the Oklahoma farm where you lived,
taking care of the youngest children. Sully,
a half-sister, that demotion—your mother dead, your father's
bride sending child after child
toward your protecting hands. "She did everything

for us," my father told us, so I saw she was their
de facto mother. She wouldn't have known
her half-relation status as anything but
bounty—her future already lodged
in her—that she would have no children.
So I hover above you, Sully,
one of my long undeclared loves, because
my father declared you in his quiet account

of having walked toward that house surrounded
by cars, the question weighing on him
as he approached: *what's happened?* Through
the door then (and now his children
with him in his telling), your black hair
as in a García Lorca play, rayed out
on the white pillow. He tells us
of your coward lover, who took you

to the quack doctor with this result. How it
quenched my child heart to suffer your
death like that. Did you guess your story
would pass to anyone as words in air,
you who were bound in the amber of your
will to help everyone around you, not
extending yourself more truly than that? If
a poem could kiss dead eyes awake, you'd

come back to me here in the house my father
built, thousands of miles from where you
were buried. And because time is both fire
and star, you'd open yourself like a music box
given to a child for nothing but delight. You'd
tell me how it is in the round of time,
to live outside it all in the beauty and sadness
your name carries when I remember

it in my father's voice each time he brought you
back to us. *Sully.* His soft saying of it—so you
are alive and dead at once—you whom
the world tried to squander, but failed

in just this dimension: that if I were to say
your name aloud in this solitary room
where my father's hammer, its exact singing,
steel to steel, came down
on every board, some air of you
might wake from the dead and speak.

Retroactive Father

He didn't get the father he
wanted when he was
a child. His father wasn't even
himself in those days. But
later, when the son didn't need
him like a child needs a father,
his father became the *good*
father. But it would never be,
man-to-man, what the son had
deserved, he felt, when he
should have had that good
father, back then. The son

was like a bank and his
memory was floor to ceiling
money. He liked to go over
with his good father all
those failed back-there-times
and watch the blue stain of
that lost past creep from
his father's fingertips to his
palms. He'd change the dye
packs from blue to purple
sometimes, but blue told
a better story. It was a kind

of solvency, don't you
see. The son accumulated
his father's debt, and even with
regret that debt could never
be paid off—just a father

running through all time
with blue hands and a son
piteously calculating his
loss. The father did not last
as long as many fathers. But
before he died he made sure
his son heard from his own lips

all his present and his back-there
missing-love. It should have been
enough, anyone would think. Still
the son walked through life
like stolen money ever after,
while his bad-good father
dug that child up again and again,
even from the grave. That story
could have no other ending.

Blue father. Blue son.

EARTH

Those dogs chuffing down black dirt
at the end of the driveway,
seeming to grin with delicious
intake—I knew earth wasn't
what it seemed. Envious, I could get down
on my knees and join their feast. Tails
wave, one paws the ground open
for the other.

The display ends as suddenly as it
began. They're off, lifted legs
marking territory. Some dogs
are only human. Yet what they did
there with their teeth and mouths stays
with me through the day. I see them as I can't
see myself, finding what they need
just under the surface—

digging for it, eagerly, letting me
wonder at sufficiency,
at certain insatiable hungers.
Needing a few bites of earth
to settle us out.

THE SEEMINGLY DOMESTICATED

cat, preens all morning
like a ballerina, caressing
its white underbelly, stretching
a hind leg into impossible
contortions, then positions
itself near the window overlooking

the birdfeeder, there to hone its
quickness to deadly ends. The door
left ajar invites it to drop its
maw of death over the greenfinch.
What it could not expect was
interception. Surprise

startles open its mouth just
that fraction needed for escape. Can
it be called a miracle to see a bird fly
from the teeth of its near
death? Skyward with ragged
desperation it gives

back more sky than it left.
The cat, its nature reasserted, takes up
its accustomed perch before
the fire on a side cushion,
reassuming its former kindly
aspect. But in the mind

of the room something free
and glad goes careening and
will not settle. Something
to do with hope, with plunder.

Wing beats coinciding
with shouts to *fly! fly!* Language itself
inhabiting the moment
with uplift.

REACHING

Eyes, mouth, hands—you've left me equipped
in your portrait *Green-Eyed Poet* with essentials, all
for moving outward, to touch, to open
what may be touched and opened. The eyes
open other eyes, have opened
hearts, hundreds of books, have met
the stolid searching eyes of the doe
in the orchard beside her fawn, teaching it to run
or stay. Fifty-three years we've shared

art and lives, with and without Ray,
whose ring of marriage is on my finger
yet. As is your right, you've turned the lapis
of his love-ring from blue
to green, to match my eyes, yet
exceeding them in that early spring promise-green.
The lips parted to the eternal "would-speak" or
"about-to-speak" or "have-spoken," the past

edging out future. The hands nest the head,
cradle the chin, anchoring the flower
of the face, otherwise subsumed
by filigree of blue tendrils. My gypsy soul—out
of which I reach for words to
carry my life and the lives of those I love—
gazes like a fountain of wonder from every corner
where your brush touches down. You know

that the soul of a poet, like blue gentian
growing alone in the forest, should never be
lifted from its incubation of shade. Providing

against this, you hide the stem, the long pedestal
of neck Modigliani might have exposed. Your life's work
forbids the soul-death of any living thing—so we are joined
in our reaching and finding, our having slept
under the same stars, wandering the fields

of our ever-emerging imaginations,
as if our vagabond natures could exact something
precious from air itself. Your poetry—of strokes,
of line and color—un-words me, stammers me
into myself like laughter in rain, so I am
lifted by your intensity out of self, by
gratitude. In every painting you bestow a democracy
of means as we gaze, remaking the world as

accessible and renewing to even the poorest of us.
What can a poet give in return—I who suffer often
the condition of word-poverty in the universe
of the ready-made?
Waterborne moonlight can lave a shore. It's
yours. Candles lit in a circle charm
and protect. I give them to you. The sky-white bay
below my window. All yours—with its ocean liners,

cruise ships, tug boats and skiffs. They are to dream
on. May a halo of hummingbirds attend you
on your walks so you'll be recognized
instantly as a deity from the Administration of
Delight for the Banishment of Misery. While I'm
at it, wouldn't you like a few golden eggs that won't
bother to hatch? And a bunch of blue grapes picked

by hands from your birthplace, Morelia? I'll also
empty my sack of about-to-be-dreams near
the basement wall that is your easel. There is
no last thing I wouldn't give you, my friend
and collaborator in the offices of *Mysteries Unlimited*.
This poem, like your portrait of me, can never
end or be finished, only pause, waiting to be seen
back into our precious continuing lives
made of light, of air.

> *for Alfredo Arreguin*
> *on the gift of his portrait of me*

RIGHT-MINDED PERSON

Most of her stories are about
getting her way, so after even ten
minutes with her you feel
you've gotten the upper hand
in your own life. You'd be exhausted
from taking her stick to the world
and hearing it whimper that way,
whack! whack! on its big

her-way butt. She has purpose and
moxie. Her head rises up like
a hen looking for the next thing
to peck. How I love those bull's-eye
moments when at least one person
is up to the task. But that's the trouble
with hen-yard justice and the rectitude
that runs it. Someone
could always show up with an axe.

I'd always walk away from
these sessions like a woman
in the '50s caught out in her rollers and
hairnet—unprepared, mortified—
her bingo stare magnetized to my
wire-sprung curls. That woman trounced
everything in and out of sight. But
if she had dreams, I never
heard of it.

IN THE TOO-BRIGHT CAFÉ

The men are comparing
killing methods for moles.
I'm ashamed to say my ears
prick up. Moles have tunneled
into my potato patch, erecting
fluffy earth-filtered cathedrals
both sides of the fence. What
are they up to down there
with my baby eye-sprouted
potatoes? They could be cousins,

potatoes and moles, each turning
the earth's darkness into something
edible or a way to thieve what light
is always holding back. Once I caught
my yard-help stomping the dirt
over their openings like putting out
underground fire. *Gas.* The collaborators
in eradication are pumping it into
tunnels as they drink black coffee
and tuck into eggs over-easy

with hash browns—"burn 'em!"
Pellets, some kind of poison.
They mull this, asking for
salsa and Tabasco. Are they
sending down heat-
seeking devices? Just don't
say "dynamite," I'm begging.
A voice by the window claims
he heard of a guy who hooked
up a loudspeaker and piped in

so many decibels the moles popped
up like mushrooms, and you didn't
have to pick them off with your
shotgun because they just kept
running. The men are laughing
by now and I'm thinking: *they're
just talking, right?* That merry
cash register by the door
is ushering a regular out, allowing
the moles a brief reprieve. The men

wave their friend onto the street
as I holster my purse. My sympathies
buzz the enormous windows like
doomed flies, those reverberating
in plain sight in the corners
where darkness will fall
and everyone above ground will
have gone somewhere to sleep
this all off. Me? I'm opening

a little café-of-the-mind where
moles can talk to flies. Intricate
labyrinths under the apple trees
and glassed-in fantasies of escape
at head-high altitudes. Moles paddling
through earth or flies foozling the air
over steak on a campfire near
the ocean. Moles will claim daylight
oxygen overrated—preferring air
filtered by darkness on the run. Flies

utter "What cute snouts you have!"
and moles have to consider life
with wings. By the time I get
home they've unionized and are
working out maternity leave and
pensions. Above it all, elk antlers
wait for tinsel and mistletoe, or
tune in to moles going on and on,
rhapsodic about ants after rain. But
because I'm the Boss, I interrupt

at the top of my smart-ass Boss-voice:
"Hey, how about a little respect!
Whose café is this anyhow?"

iv

If your time to die has come
and you die—very well!
If your time to die has come
and you don't—
all the better!

SENGAI GIBON

LET'S STORE THESE HOURS

while you are with us, but not
like a memory that says something
important is over so we look over our
shoulders to figure out what. No, let's store
your presence in our blood and breath
so when we step, you step, and we never

get to any future which puts even one of us
out of sight. Let's take hands
just to make sure. And if anybody stumbles,
we'll all stumble onto our knees
like a sudden joint prayer. You're cracking jokes
the whole time like always
because *always* is a safety zone
you carry us to when the health headlines

undermine the candelabra of the moment.
Come into our ancient cave of delight
and let us scrawl onto your heart
the graffiti of angels who favor bison and deer—
those earth signs by which any future welcome
might embrace you as tenderly
as we do. Because we are helpless with you
to hold back the days and hours

sweeping over us like a magician's cape.
You *let us be helpless together*—which
is a special gift that takes down
the night sky, like a woman taking in her wash
at dawn, spilling starlight from shirttails
and sleeves, into the dew-struck grass.

For that you will never leave us. For that
these words turn up their palms in supplication
and innocence. And to receive,
as the sea-air of words does,
every nuance of your only-ness among us.

for Jim Fisher

Season of Burnt-Out Candelabras

The sunken blossoms have melted
from the rhododendrons as surely as wax,
leaving ragged claws
the garden books advise to "snap
off." I could do this all day
—the narcotic jerk of my wrist,
the sticky juice of beauty come and
gone accumulating on fingertips,
its debris tossed to the ground like
ridiculous party hats crushed
while a lot of somebodies got drunk
and danced all night.

My hands flick stem to stem until
memories fumble my labyrinths, my
caves and alcoves. Way back
in there I remember a woman who was
gorgeous and young, who let an old man
take her to bed. She wanted to experience
everything from the inside out, and
probably there was a little alcohol
in the mix to help ambition along.
This man had a brain like Grand Central
Station, unbelievable traffic coming
and going. He was courtly, a gentleman.
She considered she was sacrificing herself
on behalf of experience, that kind of glib,

young notion. He was a great kisser,
putting everything that was slipping
elsewhere right up front so promise

crashed through to a whole other dimension
where you didn't really care if it ever
got satisfied. What a surprise! She wasn't alone
as with some of that young stuff, panting
past her like locomotives, who
left the station empty and in aftermath

leaped out of bed for a smoke. Her sweet
old man took his time. Before sex they
would have a great meal at a great restaurant
she couldn't afford. Candles would have been
lit. Music of the sultry twenties tumbled
over them like fountains alone under stars,
say in some Italian piazza at midnight,
though that phrase would never have occurred
to her then, since she hadn't been to Italy. You
could say this experience was like visiting
an exotic off-the-map island with room enough for
just two bodies. If he wanted rejuvenation,

she was sure he got it. And she?
She felt that kind of *old* that savors everything
to the last. They threw their bodies away
while they accomplished all this, and that young
alabaster cocoon of hers with skin a challenge
to velvet, became something transparent,
like the idea of never-being-old. They met

a few times like this until his reason for
being in that city took him out of even
her country and to where it was unlikely they'd

ever meet again. But somewhere now, with
age-spotted hands like mine, she could be
tossing the gaudy aftermath of rhododendron
blossoms to the plush of lawn, hauling him back
from whatever death he must surely
have had while we were both busy throwing
ourselves away on others, becoming those old
soul types who ripen young, maybe as an
unforeseen consequence of being quenched
and revived too often, before they know
much about life. It's only luck

I lived long enough to understand who
in that fated pair was doing the sacrificing.

THE BRANCHES OF THE MAPLE

have stepped back from
their white dimension, their beauty
of barren thatch forfeit to a rim of snow
holding on by its clutch
of cold. Rain in the night

changed all that, took
the laden slopes of evergreen
boughs as challenge. Seldom do
they bend so penitently
as they did this winter. Released
by downpour
they arc again toward

sky. My getting-younger
seventy-year-old friend has
returned from Burma, teaching
English to young monks. He sends
a photo of them smiling, says
they are "poor," knowing the word's
injury revised by their
delight-quotient beaming
out into the universe.

Gazing at them, the single bough
of my unburdened heart sloughs off
       its snow.

for Lage Carlson

Yet to Be Born Weather

From inside the drought
it's all we think of. Low
hanging puffy clouds,
promissory but secret
in plain sight—like
the pregnant teenager
buying Milky Ways at the grocery,

pretending to just be
getting fat.
With the weight of it,
we also are yet to be born. We
yearn and get a fever for equivalents,
suffer midnight hungers, then toss

all night trying to carry a dream
of rain into morning. Thirst allows
wild things to be called up by
the tame. Birds flock to the birdbath,
deer nose the trough left under
the apple trees. The chipmunk

scribbles itself down
the hemlock
to the half-buried tea cup
we filled from the faucet. As long
as the reservoir holds out
we can spray the inverted stars

of rhododendron petals.
We are like school buildings

closed in summer and not
reopened in September. Where
are our children's excited
voices? Where the ringing

of bells through packed
corridors? How can we be
so full and empty
at once? Trees
that endured many things
turn brown. Yet a glossy green

taunts from native salal
living on ocean fog. We
murmur like two gray voices
reduced to one injunction, both
noun and verb: *rain!*
We live only in the future now

like the ever-yielding moon
and the light-giving dying
of stars.

I Want to Be Loved Like Somebody's Beloved Dog in America

—those you see let run, let cavort on golf courses,
ears flapping—papillons, breed painted
by the masters, gazing up
like cherubs at their overstuffed mistresses
in the lounging days of other lost

empires. Bounding past flags, they orbit
the solitary figure they possess, swirl
the green knoll, not led or managed, tethered
or commanded. I know they are
fed by hand on a lap as they age; palms up

the moist offerings arrive. They pick
and choose, leaving something behind
to indicate they are aware of bounty, of the bounty
bestowed upon them, the love with its lap,
its pamper and cloy, the voice above them

at a height like a wooden flute riffling the universe—to
soothe, to mollify a beloved glance among
comets and dying suns. Theirs not to be
held like coyote or slow-eyed wolf
at the rim of the fire-circle, but

invited in, tempted by the half-picked
carcass, delivered from snarl and tear,
approach and withdraw. Still, wildness
confuses my tameness. If I scorn,
you supplicate. If I cower, you assume

my past was of the usual brutal sort that leaves
my like—abandoned. If so, let me
be abandoned in America, then sucked up
by the greed of guilt. Pull down from the high shelf
the one thousandth variety of *Bison Mixed with*

Chickpeas. Oh, America, allow me one day
of your righteous disdain
of poverty. I have a longing, a passion
to belong to something heedless and full
of mock-conscience. I might design a few

domestic habits to let it seem
I'm adjusting. You wanted a slave, a heel-licker,
and to enter the house first
with masterful stride. But I changed
all that with your beneficent rescue

of me—my pleading gaze,
as if worship came naturally to me, whereas
it plunders me, scrapes and hollows me out. What
had I hoped for in this intimate duet
to which I proffer only the arsenal of teeth

and primitive memories of a hunger
that knows how to tear
life out by the throat? And I gave that up,
for you? Caress me, my Lilliputian centaur.
I have a much-delayed appointment

with adoration, with the mercy
of your half-baked causes. Let me scratch out my
little-American-dog-will, leaving you
my rhinestone collar that used to casually strike
stars of blood against the back of your hand,

my dog tags with *your* chosen name for me, remnants
of my perpetually uncertain battleground, phone numbers
etched on them in case I should lose you, a water bowl, a coat
of fleece. Oh, America, you looked after me

so well, with your chokehold-lead and your
microchip-identity—proof of ownership
riding my neck-fat! I never had to swim for it
from a sinking boat. The heated bed banished
the roadside ditch, banished disdain,

and when I lay down near your feet
it seemed I had chosen my lot. Yet what ambition
can this level of satiety allow? The swift narcotic
of the moment tenders more than you
suspect. A small Ultimate, born out

of my loyalty, gradually arises to provoke you
to gaze past fountains and glass palisades. You
who know how to squander, put down your
pretense at wholesomeness. I am lowly
and raise you up, but to a purpose, as with all

who are helpless before might—to become
that something that thinks *in* you,

whose trusting regard works a change on you
from *inside* where you never intended
to shelter me—the one who attends

in order to interrogate, to unravel
the inoculation of your pitiful kindness-agenda.
Consider the world and its poor, its suffering—
you see how it is when something speechless
begins to think *into* you, to manifest, to bear down

on you as our double-self dissolves?
Shall we cower and beg together now? Forgive
the kick and the cage? I'm feeling tender
toward the largesse of this undertaking. "Come, Toto,"
I hear, like a last endearment before sleep. But

by then, the living-differently of sleep's velvet lining
coffins the whole of it—my plundered
ever-after heart, your incremental
changes—as those onlookers think you someone
once worthy of me—that little nothing-*Titanic*
of your sinking days.

WHILE I WAS AWAY

the piano—nothing better to do—
slipped out of key. A dull clump
breaks the tune where one
note, like a diving board bounced out
of spring by ten-year-olds, vacated
entirely. Cut me some slack,
all you things I did perfectly well
without! We've been over this before,
the last time I hyphenated
our continuum. The gone-away air brims

with sulky impenetrable remorse.
It's more than time-travel
to re-enter all this "wasn't here" as if
it were one's very own next
dimension: "whatever
happened to so-and-so?" it taunts, until
you answer, sotto voce like Bette Davis
pulling a loaded pistol
from the sleeve of her mink coat, *I'm back!*
Then rug to chair, that muffled inward:
So what—the welcome you prefer.

V

Rather than words comes the thought of high windows:
The sun-comprehending glass,
And beyond it, the deep blue air, that shows
Nothing, and is nowhere, and is endless.

PHILIP LARKIN

WITHOUT

One message mapped our days—*do
without!* It must be coded into my DNA
through a long line of chancers,
scavengers, people living on the edge.
In childhood we ran barefoot
on the face of the earth, enjoying dirt
between the toes, using those feet

like the best pair of shoes we didn't
have. Grass. The friendship of feet
with riverbanks, with the bark
of trees. Taking your feet up high into leaves
and sky—what a privilege! And teeth. Doing
without teeth. Both mother and father
toothless at thirty, teeth yanked
all at once. Pragmatic people who saw

no advantage to intermittent
pain and expense. Have a big pain if
you're going to bother with pain! They
set their false teeth afloat each night
to either side of their bed
like sentinel, macabre warning buoys,
marking the place they'd take up
their days in a kind of quiet revolution, asking
only one essential question: *what*

do we really need? Much later to live
without cars or a phone. Food
scarce for a while. Walking everywhere,
pulling belongings in a makeshift

cart. Time funnels into work and leaps
out of reach like an idiot kangaroo
hopping all over the Australia of any need-contorted
life. For when you give up things there is no
end to substitutions. The smallest

thrown-away objects can seem useful—
converting a long-dead mother's
hairpins into paperclips, or wearing
your father's trousers because they fit.
Using old things or the left-behind things
of others turns into a religion,
and if something breaks or you think you've used
it up—think again! A child in that extended family
can show you a shower curtain

decorated with butterflies
is really a tent. Take this poem—written
with the tip of a feather discarded
by a bird.

I hereby enter the sky
that floated it down to me
into my personal history of unexpected
benefactors.

Tell me, bird, what
do you need?

DEER PATH ENIGMA

Stepping where they step
in the unhindered woods
where my neighbor and I agree not
to build a fence,
I startle the lone doe
from her kingdom of solitude.

Days since she informs every hidden cavity
of fern and vine with possible
trespass—but also profound stillness
I crave when she fails
to appear. A light-footed yearning
inhabits me, though it was

blundering flushed beauty
out. I lay down
my cities, rivers bereft
of their banks, snowmelt
and downpour where she pressed
the unsurrendered harp
of her body against moss. Vaults

of cement crack open. An arbor of blustering
neon goes dark in the borderland
of word-wrecked freedoms. Out of this
overlay of the human, the doe
uncoils herself with power
that is not retreat, just
the nothing-else-that-could-happen,

as my uninhabitable shadow
triggers her fear-plundered heart.

for Jane Mead

69

The Favorite Cup

with wild horses, muzzles to haunches,
running their nowhere Western
riderless wagon-circle, has fallen to
the floor and shattered its handle. I say
it graduates to the studio as a paintbrush
holder. You ask for glue. But the handle
to anything isn't a candidate for repair.
"Put the fan-shaped ones in it," you acquiesce.

I round them up, those undaunted gazelles
of your next contentions with color
and form. If you break another cup
your false teeth can nest there while you're
dreaming. With a third I'll cut biscuits.
From there on we'll recognize our
adaptive resources—not by what's left
whole, but by how little we've abandoned.

Come fire. Come snow.
Isn't that tea water?

What Does It Say

that the only shoe repairman in town
has retired? He who mended suitcases
and purse straps. Who loved to chat
but could turn taciturn. How we laughed
over my fondness for shoes that were
clearly worn out. "Fair-weather
shoes," he pronounced like a benediction,
trying with seasons to extend

the life of my loafers. A tall man with nimble
fingers on an oversized hand, the gaze
surgeon-like. How I admired your Lazarus
revivals! For it's feet in failing shoes
that rule the world. Barefooted, we had
the ways of birds, equipped from the womb—splashing
in puddles, running after dark, bearing our troubles
and joys place to place. Addiction to shoes

came later. Whether quietly falling
apart, coming unglued, or
scrubbed down at the heels, they'd still
find a dance floor once in a while and shake
the body around to remind it how, in or out
of shoes, everything depends on the feet.
In your imagination toward repair, you gave
hope and salvage to those without money

for new shoes, or who, like me, had to
eke out their days with unmanageable feet, depending
on a makeshift tangle of sandals—a few cloth straps
stapled to a cork sole—thereby asking you to take up

the world of miracles. Shoes that had worn
themselves to feet until pain
took off its hat and stood on the curb.

You seemed to connect with us through time, cheating
it day after day, with small, momentous
restorations. And what, after all, is a world
that walks around
only in new shoes,

that stops asking for a guy like you, a man true
to this gradually
falling-apart era, alive
to our need to be treated
mercifully, our wish
to be mended and remended?

Someone to companion our fragile hopes
in the form of these emptied-out,
unsalvageable steps.

vi

For eighty years and more,
by the grace of my sovereign
and my parents, I have lived
with a tranquil heart
between the flowers and the moon.

NARUSHIMA CHUHACHIRO

BUS TO BELFAST

Where the Antrim accent
can change "heating scheme"
to "hatin' schame" or
work a shift on time with
"I'll rang you" so, in a word, it's done
as spoken.

Is, Is Not

A brief reverie while sitting at the edge
of the Pacific below Sky House,
admiring the filigree maps of wave-froth
inside the curvature as it rolls
forward, then deposits its overlay
of surrendered continents and ocean
partings into the ebb left
only moments before. Loss without
sadness! I take my restorative
like a shoreline whose surety
is always: something is coming!

~

Bird splat on the Belfast hotel
window. Then suddenly a red brush
from two stories down among beer barrels
rises like a hydra-headed dragon
to spit a spiral of courtship water
from its center. Its mating dance, like
some near-extinct bird, scrapes
the sky free of its detritus. Up and
down it prances on the tight rod
of its mission until I see better
the brick on brick my secret room
is up against. Who says
nothing works here?

~

"Pat Higgins, the Major, died right
there," Josie says, pointing to air
at the side of the road on the valley
edge. "Between one step and
the next. He was a great character,
fond of his pint, a great worker. He'd
see what there was to do and do
it without orders. He was popular."

They pray for him yet on their way
to Highwood mass, and take a blessing
for themselves at the spot where he
fell between two steps: live step, dead
step. The invisible place marked in
an invisible forever in their on-beating
hearts. Living step, dying step. Memory

                                step, no

As the Diamond

is bound by light, so are we
breath-bound into our
shining. But for that, the stone
of us would gray us past silence
into some deeper, earned
neglect. I wore a diamond once,

like a crown to a finger, but its
flash, its imperial glance had
belonged to the mother
of the beloved and would not
accept my stolen ways. Giving it
back was like trying to give back
love, or give back a mother

when her worth quenched
even the beauty of the garden
she'd left behind. Still, I am
over-attracted to the shade she
designed under the largest
evergreen, planting in formation
the stalwart deer-proof lilies

and striped hostas, those whose
petals can leech light from a cloaked
star. I swing the mattock into parched
ground, loving the weight of its dull
thud and having to claw my way
down to something gentle—as with

an Irish-moment when you realize
you will never be let in except by
holding silence until it turns
back on itself—the power of the unsaid,
an ultimate compression,
so exceeding language you banish
vast libraries with a glance away

into my hearth where blackest coal
noiselessly witnesses two wordsmiths
toiling in broad daylight by firelight,
in the glow of after-flame,
where my presence to your presence
is a humming out of which the long dead
cottage midwife, who lived here, reappears

to recount the particularities
of each parish birth, and we are thus
reborn in sparks of *first-breaths*
that ring us like a fairy fort, protecting
our held-in-light, until some
force-of-heart stuns us again
into stumbled speech and we agree

to the hostage-taking each word requires,
strung like that across the brow
of someone else's shadow-moment.
So it is when a reader opens the poem's

in-breathing—that which we took care
not to press too fully upon them
for fear we might extinguish the spirit's outlaw
vagabonding with freedom's
quarrelsome uptake.

for Medbh McGuckian

DURING THE MONTENEGRIN POETRY READING

Mira, like a white goddess, is translating
so my left ear is a cave near Kotor
where the sea lashes and rakes
the iron darkness inside
black mountains. Young and old, the poets
are letting us know that this sweltering night,
under a bridge, near a river outside
Karver Bookstore at the beginning of July,
belongs to them. They clear away debris

about politicians and personal suffering,
these gladiators of desire and doubt, whose candor
has roiled me like a child shaking stolen beer to foam
the genie of the moment out of
its bottle. The poets' truth-wrought poems drag it
out of me, that confession—that I didn't have children
because, in some clear corner, I knew I would

leave them to join these poets half a world away
who, in their language that is able to break stones,
have broken me open like a melon. Instead of children,
I leave my small blind dog, quivering
as I touch her on the nose, to let her know it's
me, the one who is always leaving her, *yes*
I'm going, she for whom I have no language with
which to reassure her I'm coming

back—what's the use to pretend I'm
a good mistress to her, she who would never
leave me, she who looks for me everywhere
I am not, until I return. I should feel guilty

but the Montenegrin poets have taken false guilt off
the table. I've been swallowed by a cosmic
sneer, with an entire country behind it where
each day it occurs to them how many are still missing
in that recent past of war and havoc.

Nothing to do but shut the gate behind me
and not look back where my scent
even now is fading from the grass. Nostalgia
for myself won't be tolerated here. I'm just a beast
who, if my dog were a person, would give me a pat
on the head and say something stupid like: *Good dog.*

CURFEW

November and a slim band of daylight
slinks through drizzle.
She has declared *No Visitors*
past ten p.m. in her cottage. She aims
to set a dish of calm before night
as it intrudes upon the mossy footpath
of comings and goings.

Instead of "Come in" she says "Not now"
and climbs the steep steps
of her hillside to commune
with anything but people. In this way
she has agitated the spirits of the place,
the villagers, an entire clan. Who
does she think she is,
assuming she can renew herself among stars?

Eddie's Steps

Flagstone set in cement,
higgledy-piggledy up the bank
to the high deck where lawn chairs
go to die in the rain. Not hard to know
these the first he'd built, set to his
stride—twice that of mine. When
I pointed this out, a sweet, startled look
came over his face, and he set to work
with a good will, slating in the extra

wedges just wide enough each foot
could advance and hold.
I wouldn't take anything for those steps,
I realized, when the visitor disparaged
them—the recalibrated provisional shifts
by which Eddie's steps accommodated
mine. The true flower
that day though was the accidental discovery

of Josie abed past noon—Eddie's "Your face looks
funny, Josie," then helping him negotiate
trousers. Gemma steadying her grandfather
to the car for the drive to hospital. But for
rebuilding my steps, they would have been
miles away in Cork, and Josie lying—speech
unraveling, steps blurring. I take my time
going up or down, feel the mind sharpen
to that day's escape. Easy now to think past
that visitor to the quiet beauty
of the climb on a dark star-filled night

when moonlight
makes its effortless way before me
all in one shining breath.

for Edward and Gemma Fitzgerald

Four-Footed

Silk napkins across our laps
like the sleeves of geisha—we eat
brown bread and salmon with capers
at the lodge on the rim
of the valley. The rumor that slurry
on fields has contaminated
local wells drifts from
our minds. Idyllic countryside

is manufactured here daily
by tourists. We crumple tea-stained
tents near empty plates,
pay our bill, then head for a walk
in a wood planted like a crop
where every tree is identical to its neighbor,
a daylight nightmare. Although

the path is marked, I fear we may
never get out. I follow you
from the dim thicket at last
into a field so open to sky
we forget the land belongs to
anyone. A woman comes out
of her cottage to stare. You wave
and she waves back as we cross

an immense distance to an iron
gate. The road downhill is no
wider than a cart, but something
incomparable has died there—
a red fox, its small perfect teeth just

visible, the blonde undercoat,
and the plume of its once airborne
tail—held in a spell now against

the ground. From the hedge
I draw out an arm's length
of wood to lift the fox-board
of our sudden death to the side,
sparing indignity. Strange how we
take voices again like two
young girls with a secret
between us, companions

now into old age and
a redundant death.

for Eli Tolaretxipi

commands a battalion of street sweepers
in Cotroceni Quarter. Car hoods,
the backs of cats, a tablecloth printed
with cherries under a cherry tree,
someone's left shoe marooned
on the sidewalk—all gilded with ochre
pollen. *Swish swish*—say the brooms
to the asphalt that once was cobblestone—
the rhythm tender as the hands
of a gigantic clock measuring its day, or

wing beats of an invisible bird
made known only as broom strokes.
I walk in gold dust with Liliana
remembering our times on these
tree-sheltered Bucharest streets—once
at night coming home, a standoff
with a pack of wild dogs: "Don't
look them in the eye!" Liliana's warning
to prevent my challenge. Now we stroll
down the center of the street like queens,

the dogs' fangs safely behind iron gates
as we pass. Who would guess how earlier
we washed our nightgowns by hand to appease
a broken washing machine, wringing dry
sleeves and hems before hanging them under
the lost blossoms of the "flying tree."
Nor would they realize we walk
everywhere on our Picasso-legs, carrying

the secret cargoes of poems yet to be
written, the gold dust drifting down,

sifting into my silver
hair. Don't mistake me—I'm still a girl
under this disguise, the one who rode
a black horse across a river in Missouri
to visit Indian caves. And Liliana, she's
still a girl picking wild strawberries
on the mountainside. Of course there's
no money for the printer's cartridge
and we write like Egyptians, everything by

hand. What is this word: "drag" or "drug"?
as we transcribe a poem into typescript.
Nothing disturbs our quiet intent to
carry words from one language into
another. Not even the white kitten's paw
swiping air as I tempt it closer with
the cherry-tree branch—its striking
and missing mirroring our eventual grasp
on each word with claws. We put down
our pens to bake a cherry pie and to speak

with Dr. Demitri, the neighbor who calls
Liliana to the open window. I notice
the crown of his gray fedora is lightly
feathered with gold dust. No one knocks
at doors on this street. Voices lift
and fall in the open air, like our laundry
breathing calmly above the kitten basking

in the garden. We let it sleep. Someone is
calling us again to the window in the glow
of lamplight. Liliana asks me to sing—

"that Irish air once more": "If I Were a Blackbird."
As I sing, the spirits of Ireland, America
and Romania join, as song binds, pours down
gold of the moment to give memory
its gilded power—that which returns us
to our most gentle, sustaining powers
of love.

for Liliana Ursu

Blue Eyelid Lifting

The stars have come onto
my pillow as they are want
to, these frigid nights
below Orion's star-slash
of welcome. I get up and
marvel with all my being.

Suddenly you are standing
behind me looking out
over my shoulder
from our back-door window
at the high display. I say aloud
the names of the few constellations

I know, told to me by my first
love. Who would have guessed
he would become our
star-bridge, he whose future
fell away from mine

in fitful times of war?
In the morning I'll unlock
the double gates to let
the workmen in, trying not to
dislodge those moments
when the blue eyelid

of unexpected closeness
pulled us in by the empty sleeve
of its far away.

for Josie Gray

vii

A raging sea
thrown from the deck—
a block of ice.

DOPPO-AN CHOHA

BUTTON, BUTTON

i

Green Peach, that's the lapel button Bashō asked Roger
Shimomura for when he spied
the "I Am Not Chinese" button Roger gave to Larry
Matsuda, as a gift at the Minidoka reunion. But, at the Irish
renga party in Stokestown following the opening
of the new wing of the Famine Museum,
a smart aleck thought Bashō's terse pen name had insulted
Greenpeace and gave him a shiner. Indeed, *Green Peach*,

the recalcitrant pith of it, was an unlikely name
for a poet. As for me, in Ireland I need a button
proclaiming me *Not a Banker*,
where honest folk lose homes daily and nationalized banks
send a country into debt while their managers
join arms in a jig singing "Deutschland Über Alles!"

Thank the Berkeley antique emporium sincerely, Larry,
for the 1960s *ABORTION NOW*
button, though I could not wear it with impunity
to the Strandhill Ballroom of Romance, even having
readjusted the baby-bump pillow in my trousers when
I glimpsed the priest and ducked
into the Ladies. There, a fourteen-year-old held out
a crisp bag, collecting spare change to get to England

on the boat for her solution. Cut marks in a ladder
up her arm had failed to convince a judge her life was
in jeopardy, her attempts so "amateurish." "Ah, you'd

have to slice a jugular, and sure, what would be
the point? You'd bleed out then and there," she sighed
and thumped my pillow as if she'd like to take a nap.
I dropped a fifty-euro note and skint past her belly,
on her neck a cameo of Savita secured by a black
velvet band. Savita, our lady killed by a heartbeat.

Savita, who took her degree as a dentist in India, then
came to die of sepsis and neglect in a Galway
hospital, an untenable pregnancy gone wrong,
her care put aside for her child's vanishing
heartbeat. "Take my child," she'd pleaded earlier,

to no avail, as she traded her heartbeat for her dying baby's
silence. *Savita, Savita,* our lady of long suffering,
who believed her death would not be required. I drop
my *Not a Banker* button into the crisp bag and Savita smiles
shyly from the girl's neck, as if she knows her husband
is taking her death all the way to the Court of Human Rights.

ii

The moon tonight is so bloated I think its mirror-moon
in Lough Arrow will pull it down. Let me wear the button
stamped *Moonbeam* all the way to the bottom.

Bashō has scribbled in my dream: "See you at Sun Ya Bar."
That dirty vodka martini I had with you there, Larry, at our
between-planes feast still beckons. But when, oh when,

will Roger inhabit the dark corner with a solitary
scotch so our glances can meet? I promise to engineer
an appearance *if* Kansas blows him our way. I could give him

some of my signature portable kisses, red as a goldfinch's
beak-rim, for his next painting. *Irish Red* let's call it,
though these finches migrate from Africa. Birds
have no boundaries and so, dear Cloud,
they don't agree to confinements, nor passports, nor
gun turrets, nor dispossessions, nor calling what was done to

Japanese American citizens during World War II anything but
words reserved for the worst injuries to spirit, body, and mind.
Maybe though, along with a concept like "concentration camp"
to recalibrate the level of that harm, we need more telling,
more stories with exact details of what was suffered. Nothing
substitutes for that. Josie is humming the opening bars of

There was an auld woman
from Wexford, in Wexford she did dwell. She loved
her husband dearly, but another man twice as well.
With yah rum dum dum dum dee-ro and the blind man
he could see!

Which song ends in a bad way for the auld lady,
so I shall turn in my moonbeam for a javelin and cinch up
my babushka for certain travail.

~

Moonbeam, we need your
accusing light: Our Lady
Savita has died.

Slow death by bureaucracy.
Civilized, remorseless.

for Lawrence Matsuda

BREATH

Frost on the glass—breathe it
open to the glass world. It
breathes back
to prove neither it
nor you can end
this exchange of breath
for worlds.

To an Irishman Painting in the Rain

He is a force against nature,
stroking stain on raw boards between
showers. Yesterday sun blasted him
free and he knew enough
to develop a bad back, though in fact,
he had wrenched it
enough for reprieve. How often

his joke during a downpour: "It's a great day,
isn't it? Let's go to the beach!" Now
between lashings of rain his brush
lavishes hope on the boundaries
of my garden. Between fresh attacks
he smokes under the eaves,
squints out across a forest to Bricklieve

as if to say: wait long enough and things
will turn, will wear themselves out.
But even hope and industry are no match
for Irish rain. Paint washes down
the white pier like rust or the teapot's
leavings. He musters a fourth coat in defiance,
as if this misunderstanding between work

and weather could be cured by holding out
against a glower of sky. Not to be beaten
he suddenly remembers an errand
and is away. Rain
washes the boards clean and is nobody's
handmaiden. Later, when the air
is mizzling against my cheeks

like cat's whiskers, I'll take in his
drowned brush, wishing always
to remember this day, on which the certain beauty
of the human will appeared to me as an Irishman
painting in the rain.

for Malcolm Gray

Encounter

Over the rain-rutted avenue
I've walked to horses at Kingsborough,
neglected estate, now plundered
by gatekeepers, the twisted arms
of rhododendron hacked for firewood. The locals'
mild compensatory salute: "It's grand
to finally see the lake!"

I hold my palm to the muzzle of a mare,
her deep eye that sinks me in,
its richly fringed lid closing over
my reflection, then lifting me
like an emissary of unknown offerings
down corridors burnished with inklings
of hounds and masters, drops of port

spilled from a flask onto her neck, or
Cromwellian plunder of silver
dug into the pasture while the horses, unbridled,
gazed on. She snuffles my empty
hand, then tosses me and history into her
farthest cavern. She'll keep me for the contraband
I am, a lonely walker who doesn't know

what she wants in a borrowed land
far from home. A small entitlement of steps
led me to mystery, seeking to be
left out. How else let difference tell you
what you are?

PLANET GREECE

He says, with mystification, the government
took a third of his dead wife's pension, she
who, fearing to lose her job, never told anyone
how tired, how depleted she felt
as her blood more and more refused to carry
her. Then one day she died, leaving their eight
children nearly grown. But she'd worked every day
and no one knew, but him, of course. He knew.

And her pension, which proved she had
worked, now leaked out of her death and over to
the government, which claimed it as his surplus,
money which sustained him when work
was scarce—the faint signal of her life blinking now
like a worn-out star in the pocket of the State.
How boldly they announce they will next take a portion
of his own small pension. What would *he* use it
for? Coal? A bit of meat? Seed for birds?

Without leaving his hearth in Ireland, he flies
through space with his country on his back. The place
he lands is rocky and chill, just like his homeland.
He sits at his hearth in a kindred field, and
spirits rise up from the ground, and the tiny hearths
of the stars take over the field of his mind.
The slow white ovens of the sheep come close. History
and governments whirl like planetary dust away

into the vastness of space. Coming in from the nightshift
at the mental home, she kisses him
as they pass in the hall, and, as in the days of their youth,
hands him, like a small kingdom,
the keys to the car.

for Madge and Josie

Cloud-Path

With steps freshened
by wearing a man's cast-off shoes,
I follow the rain-rutted road
as far as the fishing boats
turned upside down
on the soggy bank, their oars
secured elsewhere to provide
against thieves.

Mottled light through
waterside trees over the bows
and sterns means trading
fish for birds.

I take up the invisible oars
put by for just this
occasion: a banishing
scald of sun blotted inexactly
by a succession of windblown clouds
able to lift the entire flotilla.

      A bird
      flies through me. Then
      a fish.

viii

Who's singing? The one who just
a moment ago wept? Who's going to live now?
We who are dead.

JAIME SABINES

Oliver

He appears like a genie
in my sun-shattered kitchen,
ten years old going on fifty. He's
full of eagerness this first day
of his spring holidays. "I'm
coming to see you, Tess, every day!"

So he exposes any near me
for casual reluctance.
Croissants are coming out
of the oven. His timing exact.
Yes, he'll have a cup of tea
with his. He settles himself

at the end of the table like
a helmsman. Delight has driven
every shadow from not only
the living, but the dead, his
child's voice drifting out
the open doorway toward

Abbey Ballindoon and its
cache of tombstones, their
chiseled names muffled
in moss, the language
of eternity. *Tell me everything,*
my prince. Don't leave a chink

in the air. Ripple your rill
across my living heart
like a balm. We retire to

the open fire, the flames
calling out his songs, the nimble
fast ones that trot across

the brain like wild stags or
hares terror-thrilled by
hounds. We are each other's
as surely as song stitches breath
to air. But I've grown old,
forgotten the courtship rituals.

How did he learn to imagine
the strange exact gift—that
shadowed errand to Sruthlinn
Spring, kneeling there to pick
watercress to be left in a plastic
bag at my door?

"And what did you do with it?"
"I ate it," I say.
"Just like that: you ate it?"
"Yes, just like that."

The rare limestone prickly sweetness
gone into me like his spontaneous
offering of song
and, on leaving, the bright clasp
of his arms at my waist, so
I glimpse those loves in his future,
the ones who will never taste
wild watercress, the secret currency

of land-flushed water
finding its dayglow green.

And of the young letting the old
know, that memory is that other
seeping green that melds
each moment to silence until
it reappears as something else.

for Oliver Wall

A "Sit" with Eileen

It is always warm where she
is—a condition of heart. Gladness
reigns, that you have arrived to her
oblong room in which a fire burns
at an unperturbed temperature
along her left thigh. Remarks

pass on how long it's been since
you sat with her, but any yesterday
is gold today, and you easily
turn to present joys—grandchildren
coming or at hand, an outing to
a garden center, the bouquet

Marese has gathered on a side table,
she your daughter who appears now
with the plated evening meal
to be warmed later. Lassie,
the black-and-white collie-mix,
cavorts at our knees explaining

that all greetings must needs be
out of bounds and must demand
being toned down to the mannerly
thump of her tail under
the table. Fifty years we've met
like this, pouring tea, slicing cake: milk

or not, sugar or not, then mulling
times that keep those absent ones
in breath—Yvonne who, even when

we don't speak of her, seems
leaning breathless in a doorway—Maurice
forever in the photo above

the couch with a favorite
Connemara pony. (*The women of
Okinawa who live to be over 100
are singing to each other and being
attentive in small delighted
ways.*) There is mild seeking here

to see how one *really* is, what so-
and-so is doing, and if something is
amiss, a generous helping of silence
might salt it down. The snowy room
of cut glass and candlesticks
at the front of the house where

family photos keep the story entire
was given over once to the poet
as a girl, reading aloud poems
composed near the abbey, her hair,
now spiked with age.
A beautiful complicit quiet

attends as we bind up scattered
elements of the day—morning hail
that rattled gutters in shattering
sunlight, the hardworking neighbor
who cleared the ditch one day only
to be unaccountably killed

trimming hedges for the county
on the motorway. Padraig. "So
close to retirement"—as if to say
don't look for what's deserved or
expected. What comes is what
comes—our part to keep balance
with the unseen-unseeable.

Something calming in this lifting
of cup to lip, the hot tea, milk-cooled
and taken in, as if to swallow is itself
tonic, is to lean into the powder blue
of dusk, my life just next to hers

any chance it can be, which is the deep
unteachable mystery of friendship
over years. Our arms go around
each other in parting. It is profound.
I come. I go. You stay. You keep on
staying. I come again. You are here.

We lift our cups. Time is tagged
in the child's game and has to stand still.
We lift our cups. We smile over their rims
a conspiracy of *always*.

for Eileen McDonagh, and her family

Remembering Each Other While Together

Your triple bypass and plastic heart valve, my
sacrificed breast, and the boy-figure
with which your beloved passes
in and out of the room, threading the three
of us together, doe-eyed. No wonder we
are young again, though in the back-there of youth

I'm nearly killing us, plus all your potential
grandchildren, sliding in the wake of a twenty-ton
truck up the New York State Thruway in a rust-eaten
Buick. When I thought you brave, you reveal you
were only *terrified*. Remembered snow,
making us distant, drifts to either side,
forcing us down the rabbit hole of the brain's reduced

vocabulary for near calamity: *crash!*
And because we didn't, we can also remember
Edmonton, the cold Presbyterian pull of it
on a Sunday, the three of us seeking in vain
our essentials: light, music, warmth, the pint
topping out to foam, the company of natives
telling us where we were. But all was

shut, everyone tending their souls elsewhere.
Nothing to do but make our own circle
of comfort: fiddle, flute, and my invisible
instrument, listening. Our three-way promise
radiating from banishments of need—my
given-over children, your lamp-lit hearts
sworn to carry me with you, despite oceans,

continents and the twist of cultures branching us
up into the moment you hand me the tiny
smoke-blue perfume bottle that must have
been sitting for years and emptied years
on your Belfast mantel—the missing stopper,
escaped perfume—emblems of rare
infusions, when, with threat all around us,

we linked imaginations and whistled off
into our one-way dark.

for Ciaran and Deirdre

Opening

I entered this world not wanting
to come. I'll leave it not
wanting to go. All this while,
when it seemed there were two doors,
there was only one—this
                passing through.

Word of Mouth

When the dawny foal won't stand
to nurse, the vet tries his hand, but
the eye that sinks a world rolls
inward and the coiled
being, its still center, incubates
crucially, neither life nor death, but
some plateau from which
it might yet be called earthward.

That fume of breath they court lies
heavier than lead in the grass.
Some arrogance of the just-born
cripples their wills to interfere
with Nature's right to carry off
what she will. But one of them
quickens, leaves the circle
while the other horsemen shuffle,

take their voices to low registers
reserved for the "probably-not"
of any stalled creature. Armed
with a naggin of brandy, their
comrade is back to administer
a cure he heard once long ago
in his youth—that a jounce
of brandy could spark a foal

to rise out of its birth-stupor
and take legs. Wordlessly, he
bends to tilt back the newborn
head, parting the lips to splash in

the lid's worth of hope. Call it
fool's luck or memory brought
to bear on the actual, for the foal
jolts to air like a stag and pummels

its nose into the chest
of the kneeling man. His falling
backward into laughter carries
them all over the brim, and suddenly
there is a world, and they are
more in it for how that foal has
stammered itself to the mare
as the only island where brandy

turns to milk. They can go now
to other chores on the brow
of this day, having outguessed death
one more time. Words spoken
across years, suspended
in a tincture of memory, now
flushed live again as gamboling
flesh. Was it miracle, chance, or

divine favor they witnessed
on that pasture knoll? Words
stanch the goodness out
by noon and no great thing
will have happened. Still, one
scalded moment baffles,
and the day's-end ceremony
of drink at the local will spill it

night into night as wonder,
their hearts made simple enough
to believe, and all over Ireland
reluctant foals will again gargle brandy
to bruise spirits up from ground.

DAYLONG VISITOR

Had I grown up in Japan, our meeting,
my Kokeshi doll, would not have been
delayed into adulthood. I would have
carried you everywhere as I grew
steadily into your image: the mirrored
arch of brows, impish plush
of lips—their red ambush fading into
the long neck of cherry wood decorated
with feathered red-and-black designs.
All childhood did you sense my soul gone

wandering for want of your safe haven? Or
are you fled to me now,
a stand-in for one of those "day-
long visitors"—a female breath sent away
to prepare enough absence for the desired
male child? *Ko-keshi*: "child-eliminated."
Coming late to me, you eliminated
our childhood together. My soul
got used to wandering, drew energy
from wandering, drew freedom from

being alone as only a child knows how
to be free and alone. You were to have been
my soul repository from the start, if tradition
had operated as usual. But thank you
for your lateness. Whatever past you escaped
I know it was just in time, and that you
join me at this moment, an emblem
of good luck, as my Japanese American friends
intend. You've earned your keep

in their wish—you with no feet,
holding kinship with ghosts.

One day I too will have no feet and you'll
recognize me in time for the ritual
in which you'll have to be fed to fire
to unloose my spirit
as flame, as ashes and air
after smoke. But wait, little tree-woman,
let me gaze at the round, armless,
legless shaft of you—contented containment
I've fought against an entire lifetime!

Together as fire we are vigor and brightening—
then, the much delayed, unseen.

for Karen and Lawrence Matsuda

CARESS

I am like new-fallen snow.
I don't want to take a step away
from myself, as if death too
were like that, white on white
and without sign, until
the solitary heart-shaped
deer tracks catch my eye,
                    sinking in.

MARCH MOON

How unsatisfying half is
even when heading
full. Yet its shine dignifies
the bare trees

that make a lattice
for the chimney smoke
of my neighbor's
late fire. Her husband

had died before
we met, and her children
were close about her knees.
Now *they* have children.

See how many fractured and
restored moons
it has taken to make
this very half!

for Eileen Frazer

THREE STARS

looked down on me
with so much dark
between, the word
"together" would be
trespass, except for
the greater dark
that gave their light
an intimacy of
multitudes. And if

I shut my eyes, I was
a memory of
multitudes until
I opened that dark on
just those three
the instant before
they took me
in. And though
I tell you this
we are unspoken.

Writing from the Edge: A Poet of Two Northwests

I begin to think I am sometimes trying to catch up to what has happened in a time that hasn't happened yet.

One outreaches language in poetry when the in-seeing elements of consciousness ask the unseen of life to come forward. My aim has been to unseat what we assume about time, about the verities of love and death, of the consciousness of those other sentient beings next to us on the planet. We must put aside the glib assumptions we make just to domesticate our walking-around days.

The kind of poetry that seeks a language beyond the very one in which it arrives may travel from edge to edge. It is provisional and can't be too fussy about its sometimes awkward transport. In this pursuit, I find myself trying to out-leap what I can *almost* say—but that, if said outright, would utterly spoil the secret cargo that must somehow halo what is attempting to be given. I have even said that at this stage I seem to be writing in some sense *beyond language*.

I want my worlds to interpenetrate—for sky to merge with water, for fish and birds to exchange habitations so we re-experience them freshly and feel our differences, our interdependence, our kinships.

Drucilla Wall, in her essay on my work in *Thinking Continental*, hits on a central notion of my poetry when she quotes Vincent van Gogh from an epigraph in my 2011 volume, *Midnight Lantern.* Van Gogh writes: "The earth has been thought to be flat . . . science has proved that the earth is round . . . they persist nowadays in believing that life is flat and runs from birth to death. However, life, too, is probably round." This possibility telegraphs an involvement with what Wall defines as my pursuit of "an ultimate elusiveness of meaning that permeates the concept of that non-linear roundness of life, alongside the simultaneous sense of living on the edge of everything in the West."

What she sees accurately is my attempt to bind up my two Northwests: their animals, my neighbors, Lough Arrow in County Sligo in the Northwest of Ireland with the high ridge of Bricklieve and its Neolithic passage graves reaching out to America and the Strait of Juan de Fuca, the snow-covered Olympic Mountain range behind Port Angeles, Washington. My fifty-year connection to the dead of Ballindoon graveyard merges with my haunting of my late husband Raymond Carver's gravesite at Ocean View Cemetery, west of Port Angeles, where I walked every day for two and a half years while writing *Moon Crossing Bridge,* that elegy to love and loss and ongoing gifts.

~

One way to see the roundness of my life in these two places is to realize that when I situated my caravan in 1974 just outside the graveyard wall at Abbey Ballindoon to write *Under Stars,* I knew no one in that graveyard. But as recently as this past December, my companion of a quarter century, the painter and storyteller Josie Gray, passed out of this life and was buried within those walls. In mid-August, his death was followed by that of his sister, Eileen McDonagh, who had first welcomed me to Ballindoon fifty years before.

Suddenly I felt: *no wonder I immediately formed such an intuitive connection to the place to which my love would come to rest!* It was as if my 1974 consciousness already knew, in some uncanny future time roundness, that Josie was there in life and death, attached to that *as yet unlived* space and time. In other words: I had the import, the feeling of consequence, before I had the narrative, the linear here-to-there of what would happen.

I begin to think I am sometimes trying to catch up to what has happened in a time that hasn't happened yet. I am not so special in this capacity to sense a field of poetic life-abundance in places and people and circumstances. What may be special is a kind of heedless daring that trusts feelings of deep meaning emanating from a place. I take the chance that my being there has the import I feel, and I make it my life.

Just as Monet designed and grew his water-lily ponds for his paintings, I bought my cottage in Ireland eleven years ago and flew four times a year to be there with Josie. The difference between Monet's way and mine was that I just allowed the elements in that place to draw near, to inhabit me, if you will. I had no map or plan, only to be in that place as authentically as I could.

I set about knowing my neighbors, being involved with Josie's extended Gray clan, meeting painters such as Sean McSweeney and Barrie Cooke, area poets Dermot Healey and Leland Bardwell. I also drew quite a lot on my time with musicians and poets from the Republic and Northern Ireland when I was in my late twenties and early thirties.

~

Before I knew Josie, and while I stayed nights with his sister Eileen's family while writing *Under Stars*, his niece, Yvonne McDonagh, who was twelve at the time, would bicycle down to my caravan to listen to me read aloud those poems. We became confidantes, talking of love and how one might recognize it. She ultimately trained and worked as a nurse in Dublin, but sadly for her and her loved ones, died young from cancer. Still, the round of her life allowed her to marry her true love by her last year.

A story later came to me about Yvonne's death, how her favorite uncle, Josie, had caught a brown trout from Lough Arrow, cooked it, and had it carried to the Dublin hospital where Yvonne lay, unable to eat. The story goes that she found that gift so magical and such a message from home that she ate the brown trout as her final meal.

I had not met Josie at that time, but we were already bound to each other through Yvonne and a brown trout from Lough Arrow. Story must prepare the way for meaning to precede itself, to seem as if it had always been there waiting to be taken up.

So, many years later when I met Josie, he already had a sense of legend, as if our meeting had been prepared for years before by his niece's untimely death after one year of marriage. A tragedy. We were waiting for each other perhaps on opposite sides of a tragedy. And today in a graveyard where I knew no one in 1974, Yvonne and her mother, Eileen, rest not far from Josie, where I go often now to sing Josie's and my favorite song: "If I Were a Blackbird." The song is deep in traditional Irish music. It pierces time and carries us, living and dead, in the great round of our inner worlds, restoring us to each other outside linear notions of time and clearing away suppositions that would rob us of our innate capacities to belong to our futures before we even have them.

～

The complexity of a poetry that seeks to deliver liminal space and time, that which occupies a stance at both sides of a boundary or threshold, has lifted me out of easy categories as a poet. I like

Wall's locating phrase for me as having "an edge-of-everything sensibility." She posits further that if we go far enough, edging out and onward from the West, we end up in the East, that extension into the round.

My poems' ways of seeing do devolve from Eastern notions of reality. That is, they challenge dualities which tend to blot out a range of possibilities. Also, I adopt the Buddhist notion that each action we take bears importantly on the fabric of the whole, that the smallest creature, even a snail, has import—that all life is sacred and to be honored, that our path reveals itself according to our mindfulness of others and being able to see into the interconnectedness of choices.

Daily meditations, taken from a lifetime of reading Buddhist thinkers and religious leaders, are helpful to opening my mind in un-programmatic ways. One book usually in my bag as I cross back and forth between Ireland and America is *Openness Mind: Self-Knowledge and Inner Peace through Meditation*. The book is defaced with passages underlined and circled. "Try to develop a feeling for the thoughts watching the watcher"; below this I've scribbled the title of a poem I wrote later, "Little Inside Outside Dream." Or there is a question underlined in black ink: "But is there actually any 'now'?"

The seeming urgency of *now* makes it useful as a stimulus to actions which may, however, be shorn of important connections to before and after. When we consider *now* in the round of time, it is best experienced as a planet we are swiftly falling away from, but that we might re-encounter in a poem. Poems compress and expand time until the notion of *now* regains dimensionality. Such an idea of the "now" can have a past and future. It doesn't have to navigate only in the present.

~

Wall mentions ley lines of energy that are said to run through the very place in Ireland where I live, energy lines that are connected perhaps from Sligo's sacred sites to places as far away as the pyramids. She introduces the Irish term *dindsenchas*. The word means "a totality of topography, history, ecology, animal life, non-human life, spirit beings, and human impact on a place—all the living and the dead *in a non-linear simultaneity of presence.*" This passage delighted me—to discover there was already an Irish word for this complex notion of existence with which I'd been quietly working. This beautiful word carries forth a kind of poetic version of Einstein's relativity theory. It helps us stay in the round, in the deep mind I'd been drawn to in Ballindoon—for I had not stumbled upon it, but rather accepted its invitation.

When I visited the Buddhist nun Jakucho Setouchi in Kyoto in 1989 after the death of my husband Raymond Carver, she took me into her temple where she gave her legendary talks to women thwarted in love. We had instant rapport as if we had always known each other. "Why am I here," I suddenly asked at one point, feeling as if some strong, beguiling force was at work. She answered, *"Because the spirits of this place have asked for you."*

Since then I have applied that notion to my presence in the Northwest of Ireland: *I am here because the spirits of this place have asked for me.* The endeavor of my days and nights has been to see what they want with me. Their assignments are various—as simple as visiting Eileen Frazer, who gave me well water when I wrote *Under Stars.* I listen to her stories about the old days when a person entering your house would utter: "Lord give blessings on this house and all in it!" Eileen had been widowed with five children to raise alone only a year or two before we met. Her husband Jimmy, I would learn years later, had been the best friend of Josie. Now her grandson Oliver comes to my cottage to sing traditional Irish songs before the hearth—songs that connect me and my cottage to singers who've sung these songs for hundreds of years.

Another tribute I was called to make to the spirits of this place Ballindoon is the collaborative book of oral stories I took down from Josie entitled *Barnacle Soup*. In doing so, I could hear about Irish characters I'd met when they were old, but that Josie had known in their youth—such as Tommy Flynn, a fiddle player, a wit, and a *seanchai*. Now Josie rests just a few feet from Tommy's gravesite, and I walk to them both in ten minutes from my cottage.

In the strange web of things, I also discovered my cottage had been the home of the midwife who in fact had delivered Josie, a Mrs. Quinland. Last night I dreamed I was helping a pregnant woman out of bed and it felt as if I'd had a visit from Mrs. Quinland!

~

A factor that joins my two Northwests is the dependability of rain in each. I yearn for it if I am deprived of it. My sensibility seems to need it as some painters crave the color blue. I also love gazing toward the west at sundown from my Sky House or Bay St. House in Port Angeles, for there is a wide sweep of sea between America and Canada. This sea view is always changing—one minute glassy, the next white-capped by wind. Cargo ships from China and Japan, cruise ships, and tug boats pass back and forth to Seattle or to the Pacific, and a ferryboat to Victoria, Canada, sails several times a day.

There is indeed a sense of being on the edge, the edge of the Pacific Ocean, which sends the orca whales through our strait and salmon to spawn and die in rivers fished for hundreds of years by Native Americans.

The spirits of the American Northwest pulled me into small fishing boats with my father on the ocean from the age of five. Fishing teaches patience and the unknown, the unseen. Light illuminates the mind on water and the motion of the boat is a lullaby. It is a natural state of meditation. Speech on deep water is changed and intimate. The mind drifts. Things of a trivial nature lift away. Life seems bared to essentials. When one is on the ocean, one feels in touch with sacred space and non-linear time, that wistfulness toward simultaneity of times and places.

My childhood was spent in the logging camps where both my mother and father made our living, she as a choker-setter and he as a spar-tree-rigger. While my mother and father were felling trees, I was exploring with my brothers, building shelters, making trails, picking wild berries, tracking bear and deer. I was also always on the verge of getting lost in the greater forest.

It was all perhaps a preparation for becoming a poet—surrounded by the unknown, daring to venture, to pass back and forth from the wild to the domestic of home and hearth, all the while watching the larger-than-life efforts of my parents as they risked their very lives to earn a living from the forest.

~

Being with forests and oceans allows one "extremes of other-than-human domains." Wall says these connections in my poetry offer "a radical form of empathy that is not simply local and not absently, abstractly global."

In these exchanges, passing back and forth between my two Northwests, I leave hummingbirds and eagles in Port Angeles for goldfinches, mute swans, and wild pheasants in Ballindoon. I leave deer, black bear, cougar, and bobcats on the Olympic Peninsula for badgers, foxes, and elegant stags with their regal racks of horns in the West of Ireland.

I assume some cross-pollination of empathy and attentiveness must be taking place through bringing these disparate inhabitants together in one consciousness. In the process, and through my poems, I feel I am being transformed from the inside out.

TESS GALLAGHER
ABBEY COTTAGE AND SKY HOUSE

Button, Button: This poem was written over a four-year span as part of a larger collaborative exchange of poems between Lawrence Matsuda in Seattle and me in the Northwest of Ireland. Because there are so many cross-cultural and political references, I offer the following notes:

Green Peach: the first pseudonym Bashō took for his writing.

The Famine Museum: at Strokestown Park, Strokestown, Co. Roscommon, Ireland. It is located in the original Stable Yards of Strokestown Park House. It was designed to commemorate the history of the famine of Ireland and in some way to balance the history of the "Big House." The Great Irish Famine of the 1840s is now regarded as the single greatest social disaster of nineteenth-century Europe. Between 1845 and 1850, when blight devastated the potato crop in Ireland, in excess of two million people—almost one-quarter of the entire population—either died or emigrated. I visited the museum with my niece Rijl Barber and Josie's daughter Siobhan Gray in 2016, and it made an indelible impression on me, how great the suffering of the Irish people has been.

The National Anthem of Germany: composed by Joseph Haydn. This reference recalls the famously reported Anglo Irish Bank's former manager's singing "Deutschland Über Alles" in a taped phone conversation with former chief executive of the bank

David Drumm in September 2008. The managers knew that the billion-euro aid package from the European Union would not be enough to save Irish banks after the collapse of the Celtic Tiger. That's why they swore about naive German savers who would ultimately foot the bill, before singing the first verse of the song "Deutschland Über Alles," cynically making use of the German people's propensity to save.

Crisp bag: Here the reference is to the fact that women who became pregnant in Ireland before May 2018 and who sought an abortion for any reason (rape and incest were not reasons for abortion under the 2013 limited abortion law) had to travel to England to obtain one. They usually travelled by boat. Therefore, they had to find round-trip passage fee, accommodation in England prior to the procedure, plus money for the abortion and also aftercare. The woman in the poem is suffering this plight. That she is collecting money in a chip bag is an ironic indication of her desperation and humiliation.

Limited Abortion Law: In Ireland the question of whether a woman threatening suicide, because she is pregnant, would be allowed an abortion was brought forward during the vote for the so-called "limited abortion law" which passed on July 12, 2013. Under this restrictive legislation, one doctor was required to sanction an abortion in the case of a medical emergency; two in cases where there is a physical threat to the life of the pregnant woman; and three—including either an obstetrician or gynecologist and two psychiatrists—where there may be a risk of suicide. By an overwhelming vote in May 2018, this amendment was overturned and a new bill approved which would allow abortion to the twelfth week.

Savita Halappanavar: an immigrant from India to Ireland, died in University Hospital Galway on October 28, 2012, from multiple failures in treatment, but also because confusion over the anti-abortion law became a "material factor." She had been hospitalized with an untenable pregnancy. However, under Irish law at the time, the life of an unborn fetus was to be sustained before the life of the mother. The baby's heartbeat had to stop before it could be removed from her womb. Savita Halappanavar subsequently died of sepsis due to inattentiveness to her own care during this doomed pregnancy. There were worldwide protests in India, Great Britain, and Ireland. A full inquiry found that she had died as a result of what was ironically called "medical misadventure." Her death became the stimulating factor in reconsideration of the effect of the anti-abortion law in Ireland. In fact, it has even been suggested that the May 2018 law that revised the 2013 law be called Savita's Law. It allows abortion up to the twelfth week, with other considerations governing abortions after that period.

Sun Ya Bar: famous bar located in the Seattle International District formerly attached to the Sun Ya Restaurant. Roger Shimomura, the famous Japanese American painter, frequented it and also occasionally other poets, writers, and artists. Mike Seeley gives a rich description of this Seattle landmark:

> *At 4 on a Tuesday afternoon, the bar is half-full but pregnant with promise. Every patron is on the wrong side of 40, with blacks and whites peppered (or salted) among a mostly Asian crowd. Three television sets of varying sizes show Hurricane Isaac hitting Louisiana, Asian art adorns the walls, and red paper bulbs hang from the black tile ceiling, muting the lights. Against the back wall rest a wood stove and dartboard, both out of commission, and swivel chairs make for a potentially great bout of bumper drunks. The Bartender: Tall, dark-haired Gloria Ohashi boasts a deep voice and quick wit. A skinny regular comes in and*

hands her a small green pumpkin that he says he found on the bus. "We don't have regulars," says Ohashi. "We have lifers." Seattle Weekly, Sept. 11, 2011, by Mike Seeley.

"The Old Woman from Wexford": (also known as "Eggs and Marrowbones") is a traditional Irish folk song that, like so many old folk songs, has origins lost to history. It's a humorous ballad, wherein an unfaithful old woman is taught a lesson when her blind husband steps aside and she plunges into the lake instead of her pushing him in, as was her design!

ACKNOWLEDGMENTS

"Ability to Hold Territory" appeared in *The Plume Anthology of Poetry* (Volume 6), February 28, 2018.

"Almost Lost Moment" appeared in *Plume*, February 2018 online edition.

"Ambition" was first published by the *New Yorker*, 2019.

"Button, Button" first appeared in *Boogie-Woogie Crisscross* written in collaboration with Lawrence Matsuda, published April 2016 by MadHat Press.

"Blind Dog/Seeing Girl" and "One Deer at Dusk" appeared in *Mānoa*, 2012.

"Cloud-Path" was first published by the *New Yorker*, February 6, 2017. Also in *Get Lit! 20th Anniversary Anthology*.

"Deer Path Enigma" appeared in *Washington 129*, an anthology of Washington State poetry, 2017, edited by Tod Marshall, Poet Laureate of Washington State.

"Earth" was first published by the *New Yorker*, February 5, 2018.

"Encounter" and "As the Diamond" appear in the anthology *Thinking Continental: Writing the Planet One Place at a Time*, University of Nebraska Press, 2017, edited by Tom Lynch, Susan Naramore Maher, Drucilla Wall, and O. Alan Weltzien.

"Hummingbird-Mind" appeared in *Stony Thursday No. 16*, Summer 2018, one of the longest-running literary journals in Ireland.

"I Want to Be Loved Like Somebody's Beloved Dog in America" appeared in *Metamorphic: 21st Century Poets Respond to Ovid*, edited by Nessa O'Mahony and Paul Munden, published by Recent Work Press, Canberra, 2017.

"Oliver" appeared in *Narrative Magazine* online, Spring 2016.

"One Deer at Dusk" appeared in *Catamaran Literary Reader*, Fall 2018.

"Opening" and "Recognition" appeared in the *Sun*, 2018.

"Reaching" appeared in *Alfredo Arreguin's World of Wonders*, Cave Moon Press, 2018.

"Stolen Dress" appeared in *Poetry* in 2019.

"Three Stars" appeared in *Plume*, April 2018.

"To an Irishman Painting in the Rain" appeared in *Catamaran Literary Reader*, Winter 2014.

~

Section Quotes: *Japanese Death Poems: Written by Zen Monks and Haiku Poets on the Verge of Death* became especially important to me during my cancer battle from 2002 onward. It was compiled with an introduction and excellent commentary by Yoel Hoffmann, and published in 1986 by Charles E. Tuttle Co., Inc.
   Specific quotes within the above book are:
   Section ii: *Give my dream back . . .* by Uejima Onitsura, p. 251.

Section iv: *If your time to die has come* . . . by Sengai Gibon, p. 74.

Section vi: *For eighty years and more* . . . by Narushima Chuhachiro, p. 77.

Section vii: *A raging sea* . . . by Doppo-an Choha, p. 153.

Other section quotes in order:

Section i: *Am I real* . . . by Osip Mandelstam, translation by Robert Tracy, from *Stone*, published in the US by Princeton University Press, 1981; Harvill UK edition used, 1993, p. 93.

Secton iii: *I hate Batyushkov's arrogance* . . . by Osip Mandelstam, translation by Robert Tracy, p. 105.

Section v: *Rather than words comes the thought* . . . by Philip Larkin from "High Windows" in *Collected Poems*, edited by Anthony Thwaite, published by Farrar, Straus and Giroux, 1989, p. 129.

Section viii: *Who's singing?* . . . by Jaime Sabines, translation by Philip Levine and Ernesto Trejo, from *Tarumba: The Selected Poems of Jaime Sabines*, published by Sarabande Books, 2007, p. 103.

~

Irish artist and storyteller Josie Gray, my companion of a quarter of a century, sustained me with wit and delight in each new painting and story. His passing on December 19, 2017, before he could see my book bearing his painting and my dedication adds another reaching to my efforts here. Our singing to each other by the fireside in my cottage in Ballindoon, Northwest of Ireland, is the undertow of music these poems bear for me.

Many thanks to Alejandro González Iñárritu, great director and friend, for giving me the work of the Mexican poet Jaime Sabines. And for his incomparable friendship which companions me deeply.

143

Abiding support comes always from enduring friends Dorothy Catlett (her late husband Dick), Alice Derry (her late husband Bruce), Lawrence and Karen Matsuda, Alfredo Arreguin and Susan Lytle, Greg Simon (who midwifed this book), and his wife Helle Rode; Holly Hughes and John Pierce, Jill Ginsburg and Louise Clark, Jeffree Stewart, Tim and Debra Roos, John Hamrick (his late wife, Nita); Ann Elizabeth Fisher and her late husband, Jim Fisher; Howard Chadwick, and Harold Schweizer. The late poet extraordinaire Lucia Perillo graced me with friendship over thirty years. Jane Mead's friendship and poetry span my life with Ray and Josie. Tony Hoagland's wit and unequivocal intelligence blazed forth in my University of Arizona classes and grew to irreplaceable dimensions for all poetry, not just American poetry. Joan Swift's friendship and extraordinary poetry were a mainstay and a privilege, since our classes with Theodore Roethke at the University of Washington in 1963.

Both my American and Irish families have been good to understand and put up with my crucial hyphenations, when the hummingbird-mind of writing stole me away at intervals.

My Irish grandchildren and great grandchildren by way of Josie contribute the long arm of the future—Gemma Gray Fitzgerald, Edward Fitzgerald, Brian Questa, Karen Gray and her children Jade and Lee; Megan and Eithna Boyle with her Abbey; Brendan and Collin Cunningham.

Two Eileens, my neighbors in Ballindoon—the late Eileen McDonagh heard my early poems in her cottage parlor in the early 1970s, and Eileen Frazer gave me well water for tea during the writing of *Under Stars* next to the Abbey Ballindoon just steps from my own Abbey Cottage. Without their sustaining welcome over more than fifty years, this book would not have been possible.

Friendship with Oliver Wall, a young Irish traditional singer, allows me to reach back into time, when I travelled both the North and Republic of Ireland with musicians and poets. The tradition of singing before the hearth, which so preserves the Irish past, is greatly alive in Oliver himself, and places my cottage wondrously in that past, then carries it over into the present and future.

Irish friends and family, Marese McDonagh and Brian Farrell, have taken me out to Irish music, shared walks around Ballindoon, and invited me to sit before their hearth with Eddie and Sadbdh, their children. Paula Gray drove me to Spiddal, from where my mother's family, the Morrises, hail.

Dymphna Gray, a friend for over fifty years, without whom I would have no Irish life, graciously continues our London friendship when we worked in the Dress Circles of several theaters. If she had not suggested I meet her sister Eileen McDonagh—no Ballindoon, no quarter of a century of life with their brother Josie!

Jimmy Frazer who ditched his field to save my cottage from flooding more than once, but crucially in spring of 2018.

My two American nieces, Rijl Barber and Laurie Ellison (her daughter Lilly and son A.J. and husband Tom), visited me in Ballindoon August of 2016. In 2003 my nephew, the poet Caleb Barber, accompanied me to Ireland. These visits, along with those of Jay and Raku Rubin, Jan and John Harrington, and Louise Clark with Jill Ginsberg, helped stitch my American life to my Irish sojourns.

My Irish "daughter-in-poetry" as we claim for each other, Medbh McGuckian, visited Abbey Cottage summer of 2015 with her son Liam. The poem "As the Diamond" celebrates that visit and her own matchless poetry.

Ciaran Carson and Deirdre Shannon Carson have been central to many welcomes in Belfast City, a place where many of my inner notions of music and Irish poetry and, indeed, Irish life were formed.

The Dublin poet, Nessa O'Mahony, and her writer-cinematographer husband, Peter Salisbury, have been supportive friends in visits both in Dublin and at my cottage. Peter's wonderful documentary, *At the Ballindoon Café*, on Josie Gray, celebrates his painting on josiegray.com.

Liliana Ursu welcomed many of these poems into her Romanian for their publication in September of 2017 in *The Gold Dust of the Linden Trees*.

Hiromi Hashimoto, my Japanese daughter-by-heart-adoption, has been a responsive and companioning spirit for many years. As friend and translator she is purist gift to my work. Each visit is a pure oasis.

Vicki Lloid, choreographer and friend, from Walla Walla, Washington, has set poems by Raymond Carver and myself in dance arrangements over the past twenty years. Her latest dance uses "Blue Eyelid Lifting."

Pat Henry and his wife Mary Anne, colleagues from my teaching days at Whitman College, have inspired me with their projects—especially Pat's *We Only Know Men: The Rescue of Jews in France during the Holocaust*.

Laurie Lane of Fox Island—who is my driver and boon companion going and coming from airports and ferry crossings while traversing great ongoing conversations about poetry and life—deserves mention for her faith in me, her smiles, her can-do, "I've got your back" kindness!

Danielle Vermette, who bent over this manuscript like a mother, cherishing me and the lives of those I carry. Her continued support during and after the death of my companion as I crisscrossed from America to Ireland, then in April sidetracked to Spain to lecture, has been an incalculable gift! Her wit and deep corridors of understanding have kept me going.

Bounteous thanks to Katie Dublinski for the exceedingly close attention she has given each element of this book. She is nothing short of amazing.

Jeff Shotts, steadfast editor for most of my books at Graywolf, has again helped make this book come together in what I believe to be its best form. His vision, good judgment, and attentiveness continue to guide and inspire me.

Alice Derry, my dear friend and neighbor on Deer Park from times with Ray onward, deserves highest mention as my companioning poet, who often shares meals, walks, and her poetry with delight and sweet readings aloud to me. We are each other's mainstays!

TESS GALLAGHER is the author of ten previous volumes of poetry, including *Midnight Lantern: New and Selected Poems, Dear Ghosts,* and *Moon Crossing Bridge.* She is also the author of four collections of short fiction, including *The Man from Kinvara: Selected Stories* and *Barnacle Soup: Stories from the West of Ireland,* a collaboration with Irish storyteller Josie Gray. She has also published two works of nonfiction, *Soul Barnacles: Ten More Years with Ray* and *A Concert of Tenses: Essays on Poetry.* Her poetry has been translated into Spanish by Eli Tolaretxipi (*Amplitud,* Ediciones Trea, 2015) and Romanian by Liliana Ursu (*Pulberea de auro a tailor,* Baroque Books & Arts, 2017). She worked with Alejandro Iñárritu on *Birdman,* and Robert Altman named her "a real contributor" to his *Short Cuts,* both films based on stories by her late husband, Raymond Carver. She spends time in a cottage on Lough Arrow in Co. Sligo in the West of Ireland, and also lives and writes in her hometown of Port Angeles, Washington.